I dedicate this book to my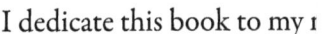

Vanilla Gods

Tamara Mushani

Published by Tamara Mushani, 2024.

While every precaution has been taken in the preparation of this book, the publisher assumes no responsibility for errors or omissions, or for damages resulting from the use of the information contained herein.

VANILLA GODS

First edition. June 30, 2024.

Copyright © 2024 Tamara Mushani.

ISBN: 979-8224892181

Written by Tamara Mushani.

Godless and looking

Early in the morning,
as the sun takes on its climb,
I marinade in feelings of unworthiness
like honey, it sticks to me
but there's nothing sweet about it
if everything beautiful had its opposite
this is what it is
bitter, foul taste of reality
played over and over again
and sadly,
stingingly true

VANILLA GODS

I've been battling with this thought
since i was eight
and still now at 23, i struggle with it, too
and something tells me that i will be struggling with it
some years from now, too
even worse than i am now
with all the expectations society puts on the aged
i am not enough
i don't think i ever have been

sleep,
because it means i get to run away from myself for a bit
sleep,
because for a while, i am not myself
sleep
because suicide is too permanent a thing
sleep
because i'm afraid to hurt others in my self-termination
but sleep
because that's really what i want to do
to wake no more
to try no more
to just sleep

the dishes have been washed
and are left to air-dry on the rack
in the room, sits a book to be read
the clock is ticking
and smiles mockingly at me,
you're aging
still no lover to share your bed?
girl, soon you will be dead.
this thing of finding someone to understand
is getting dire
because it makes you feel like you're a road with too many
twists and turns
in a world where people prefer to cruise the highway
and smooth roads
it's easier people to pick up there
girls who smile and comb their hair
billboards showing the perfect woman in her silk underwear
perhaps it was my childhood
that's what made me this way
complicated, emotionally unstable,
fearful
i don't know let's find anything to blame
for the person i have become
who asks for a room for understanding
when really i know to deal with me, i should probably request a mansion
the clock is ticking
its hands are a smile
go back to your little room
and read for a while
like you always do, sweet, lonely child
i could have cried for 365 nights

the nights i did not,
i was too drunk to
that's how i survived
the hell i was thrown into
grief is like inhaling some gas
that slowly burns at your insides
while you consciously await your death
it's painful basically
i cried for 365 nights,
apart from when i drank to hurry me to a sleep
i wished was my death
i cried for 365 nights
and i'm crying still

VANILLA GODS

i run away from myself
in sleep
in alcohol
in sex
in talking
anything to not be with this demon
that is called Me

fucked up
describe yourself in a phrase
these are my go to words
that can't be healthy
how did i end up here
not fucked up, i mean
i mean thinking of myself in that way
maybe because you are
another voice says
i just can't seem to get it right
things, that is
everything i do,
i make a mess
i try to explain that to a lover
who i am, i have to confess
because i feel like an impostor
when i spend all this time with you
when i know who i really am
deception
sometimes, i deceive myself for a moment, too
only to come back to that little phrase
describe yourself
i am fucked
up
and i am not going to waste my time
explaining to you why
just to see that look, you agree, it's all in your eyes
sigh upon sigh
lie upon lie
fucked up
not for a minute
or just today

but all the fucking time

the first time i washed my hair on my own
retouched it, as we call it,
i felt as though something wrong had happened
wasn't this too soon?
or was this really where life was going?
it then dawned on me
someday, i will be alone
i was used to my mother doing my hair for me
but in the last months,
she'd grown sick and so i had become accustomed
to doing things around the house myself
but my hair, that was something different altogether
at first, i had gone to salons when she fell ill
recoiling at the touch of another but mother's hand
but one night,
it had come down to it
i had to do it myself
i sat down, used to crossing my legs,
as i had done as a girl,
and was confronted with my face in the mirror
you are doing your own hair
mama's gentle hands aren't going to run themselves through
your DNA which is her DNA,
and part the courseness,
they are not going to spread the yellow mayonnaise all through it,
and then comb through it
you will return from the shower
hair wet, knowing that you will not be putting your head
in between her thighs as she holds your restless head
in place
you will turn that blowdryer on and adjust the heat
as you see fit

it's your hands now
which sit at the end of your arms
attached to your body
you doing this on your own
no other soul
never have i felt so alone

i called you into the shower
whilst i stood under its waters
and you came
you undressed then joined me
i handed you the soap
and smiled
you took it from me
and then began laughing at the music i listened to
whilst in the shower
i laughed with you but
the sad thing was that deep in my heart
as romantic as the moment seemed
i knew i didn't love you and that the moment was a deceit,
i never could as much as i had tried
but you looked at me like you were having such a good time
so, i left the shower first
and pulled the shower curtain behind me
and left you to clean yourself up
i wanted to add before i left,
'wash yourself thoroughly of me, so that you can forget me'
because when you leave my front door,
i will have forgotten you

VANILLA GODS

I knew that maybe I was fucked
when I bought a bottle of gin
took it home
and drank it all in one night alone
to numb myself against
the new pain you dealt on me
I'd never felt pain like that
the kind of pain
that made me ashamed to call on God
Or anybody for that matter
to see me so weak
so small
so lost
I had leaned on you
and then made you the foundation of everything
and when you decided to pull yourself out from under me
after I had given everything
man, I needed to escape
that icky feeling
that disturbing feeling
that disfiguredness
when would i be able to look in a mirror again
so i filled my blood with alcohol
hoping i could be cleansed of your touch,
your smile, your laugh, the way you drove that car
me in the passenger seat, your hands, your thoughts, your voice
all of it
you were my illness
and for those few days, that gin was the medicine

gin is clear

water is clear
gin smells potent
water hasn't a scent
but somehow, i mixed the two
8 glasses of gin
does the trick
to make me not me for a little while
if it's not that, then sleep
and there you have your remedies for a broken heart

VANILLA GODS

I pray to God
you never watch your lover love someone else
rather some disease
or ill treatment
or a fall from a mountain top
but I pray to God
you never see your lover look at someone else
and say they are their world

For the longest time she couldn't think
She thought you would come back to her
to us
that you'd love how people should love
that you wouldn't be as cruel as you were
once, long before we had escaped her womb,
you loved her, touched her,
laughed with her,
then there was this darkness
and you never did
was your cruelty maybe a madness
maybe you were a mad man
because nothing can explain
why you treated a gentle, loving woman
the way you did
she'd still clasp her hands together though
in the dark of night
and ask the Heavens to bring you back to her
and that's what I could never get
in love, are you meant to lose your head?
to a point where you cannot even discern that
that love is in fact not love at all

VANILLA GODS

I was angry
Angry because I saw him cry
Angry because I needed something from him
and again, it couldn't be satisfied
Angry because I needed an object
was treating him like an object
at which I'd lash, and have all these hateful
thoughts towards, pent up shit, all projected on him
then I saw him cry
over something that happened in his life
and I was left to again see that he was just another human being
With his own thoughts, emotions, rights, needs
His destiny was not to heal me
or be some mirror at which I could throw my own frustrations at
He was a person
And I was going to have to heal on my own before causing
another person pain they didn't deserve
So, I took my angry ass home
Closed the door
And wailed

I wish you could have been the man that you are now
when mom was still around
She deserved a good man
And that, since you're moving closer to the grave,
or aging or whatever,
is what you're becoming now
You must have put thought to it
But I wish you were this man now
back then
The man that comes home early
And cares for paying bills
And wants to sit around his children
And cares for belonging to a community
I wish you were this man
that puts thought to things like compassion
and empathy
Who thinks before he acts, or even talks
I wish you could have been this man
when we all needed it
Because now we're grown
And all I can remember is the man you once weren't

VANILLA GODS

You've got to take your ass home
To a quiet room
And heal
You've got to take your ass somewhere
for a long walk if home is rowdy
And heal
You've got to heal on your own
Before you cause damage to the world with
all your demons

I remember the evening sky was bruised in dark purple
And he just learnt there was a death in his family
And I had come to learn that we are all people
Going through our own shit
So I'd have to become accustomed to dealing with
my own shit, too
And instead of thinking of him with such inhumanness
I'd have to accept that what I do to him I do to me
Because we're all going through it

VANILLA GODS

Sometimes, I think myself far deep into
a darkness
That I'm left to sit with my head in
my hands
and think why girl, why do you do this?
Why do you kill yourself over and over?
Why do you put this bullet to your head
only to have to clean up the mess yourself
and then do it all over again?
And the truth is that I can't help it
To think, to have this mind that is so
used to the dark.

You don't know the strength it takes
to visualise yourself every night
at a sink of blood
that is your own
a razor on the floor
dropped from your weakened hand
to see yourself going
finally going from this place
to which you were sent
and endured a miserable existence
finally going
to see yourself so clearly leaving
and not do it
and the next night see it all again
and still not do it
every night, you see it
and don't do it

VANILLA GODS

I must learn to stop feeling so sorry for people
and accept that people choose to get themselves
into the messes they end up in

It's days like this
when I feel useless
when I so badly want to run
to another
place myself under their body
sex
is some kind of thing for me
which I know it shouldn't be
but something about another person needing me
for their pleasure
to feel so good
makes me feel worthy again

VANILLA GODS

Sometimes, I sit awhile
and I realise it all so clearly
It's a bunch of bullshit
caring what other people think of how you look
caring for work that will end once you're in the grave
for spaces where you will easily be replaced
so artificial
then the moment flees
and I am back in the race of it all

I sometimes sit in a group of people
and play this game called who is the most fucked up of all of us
and sadly, usually I win
and i always think fuck, how fucked up am I

VANILLA GODS

I watched you play with dolls
And watch animations
Then outgrow them and become into other things
I watched you sleep, saw how the light of dawn came on your face
Had my face buried in your messy hair as we slept meant to be pillows apart
But came close in the cold of the night
I watched you brush your teeth with toothpaste
Foaming at the mouth
And then eat your scrambled eggs with a mouth open as we talked about what we were going to do throughout the day
And then us looking at clothes later in the afternoon
What we will wear
I watched your small breasts grow from nothing into something
And compared them with mine
And laughed at our beestings
I watched you stand in the line at the cinema, eager for the movie we will see
And saw you put butter in your popcorn and sour cream, so much sour cream and chives
And I did the same because we liked the same things
I watched you drink your slushie and get brain freeze from the ice
We then split the chocolate in half
I watched your eyes change as they adjust from the dark of the cinema to the light of day
Or all the lights of the mall if it was then night time
I heard your name be called from my mother's mouth as though you were one of her own
You became my sister
I watched you as you talked about boys
Or things you loved
Or the career you intended on pursuing

I watched you as our weekends faded and it was time for another week

I watched you get in your mother's car

And she'd wave me hello and we would smile at each other because of all the secrets we knew that no one else did

I watched you for 16 years

And in one, I had to move away, and now you've decided the distance will win

You know I've had pain in my life

I've had to grieve before

At least you could have let me not grieve you, too

But I guess not

Because I guess you decided

And now I don't watch you anymore

Losing a best friend
isn't like losing an arm
but like losing your heart
I thought I knew pain until I
learnt losing a best friend
They're still in your dreams
And in your dreams, you're still
doing all of these cool things you used to do together
But you wake up, and that's no longer the case
They're gone
And you must now grieve a terrible grief
to which you wish to run away to sleep in
but there, you only dream again
sweet dreams aren't sweet when you wake to a bitter reality

I learnt that people do not think of death
as much as I do
well, that's what some people told me
It just makes sense to me to contemplate this other state of being
to which we'll all go a little harder
every time I do, it's like I ironically die a little
and then come back as something different
Truth is, I think we all think about death
Just a lot of us don't want to acknowledge we do
Because once you do, you're left to think of how small you really are
How you have no control over anything
and no idea why you're here
and that can all be really frightening

VANILLA GODS

I know you think you gave your all to loving me
But to me it was nothing
Far from enough
And what worries me is that if you think that was your everything
then how lowly you must think of me
how love must be some ordinary thing to you

I want to be loved by other people the way I love other people
I wonder why no one can do as I do
Why I should always be the one putting in great effort

VANILLA GODS

Godless
and on the bathroom floor
it's nearly midnight
and I am so lost
so stuck
Empty
Lifeless
How will I get out of this

I am in the backseat
On the road to nothingness
Driving is cynicism
and quite frankly,
A driver who took so long to
learn what responsibility is
But I have to sit in this car
Because he fathered me
Sometimes I fear we'll crash
I fear that all the anger I have will explode
and take over
And kill us all
So I try sit as small as one could possibly be
In the backseat as hell plays outside my window

Stupid love
Crazy love
Tough love
Hardened love
Bruised by love
Afraid of love
Tough love
So hardened up
Difficult to trust
psychotic love
Abused by love
Burnt by love
Identity lost
Disassociated a lot
Traumatic love
Given up on love
Mad love
Sick love
Twisted love
Never cared for us
So goodbye love
I've had enough

Stay away winter sun
You are a half-promise
A wasteful servant
A tired lover
Unfaithful friend
Weakened in purpose and resolve
Leaving me alone and bitterly cold

VANILLA GODS

I have arched my back for men
Opened my legs, split thigh from thigh,
Moved an angle to the left or sat up better
To receive men

I have had men put themselves over me, onto my belly or my lady parts,

Felt its warmth and wiped it with a tissue or sometimes slept in it before washing myself with a shower in the baptizing light of dawn

I have come to learn that men are not entirely magnificent or not magnificent either

I have come to learn that men have a strong obsession and desire for power

All men want it, want to be seen and treated like they are the only one in the world

The light of dawn came in and he woke me
'It's time to go.' He said.
I was amazed. No breakfast in the morning?
Or a cup of coffee. Or a few more hours to at least sleep?
I really was just a spread of the legs.

The security guard looked at me with pity as I stood outside waiting for my taxi.

Simply put – chased from a house.

I got home and realized I had dealt myself a portion of harm.

I had allowed myself to be treated so lowly by someone who would never be able to comprehend my worth and didn't care to.

I slept that morning wondering what the sex was for him.

Perhaps it was good. I was too drunk to even remember it.

SEX
A three lettered word
Through which my soul has travelled
And cut itself

I make love to a man that I hate
And he doesn't know it
I unfold myself before him
Smoothen out the creases of my self-loathing
To make myself a little more presentable for him
Tonight, I couldn't have gin to numb me out
I guess I will just have to fuck consciously
Oh, Mary, who conceived without sin
Look at your daughter
Look at me
Close up the heavens
Take the light of the stars
Let no eye witness
The demon within me moving
The dead girl on her back
As I make love to a man that I hate
And he doesn't know

VANILLA GODS

I held your hand
and it was warm
you then pulled me into your body
and it was warm
you then kissed me
and your kiss was warm
I flinched
what's wrong? you asked.
warm is a little hot for those of us used to the cold

I bent down, at the waist,
and hunched over, caught my breath
it was finally catching up with me
I had run my whole life
from myself
from the experience of these lesser emotions
until something sent a cloud
that breathed over me
'stop running and face it'
so, I first bent down, caught my breath
then turned around
and screamed
and my cheeks were wet
from the clouds or myself
i couldn't tell
but something told me it was going to be like
this for hours
but most importantly, that was okay

VANILLA GODS

Now that I think about it
I have lived through many depressions
and at the time didn't know I was depressed
In my teenage years, all I knew was that I
was so sad and anxious and nervous,
but I didn't know it was severe depression
and maybe anxiousness
I just thought that one day I will want to get
out of bed
That one day, I wouldn't feel so nervous
about anything
That one day, I wouldn't look at the rain
and wish it could wash me and my blood away
That one day, I would be okay again

the woman walks early in the morning
off to work
as I'm off for a jog
the smell of sweat clings to her armpits
the sun has not even risen
hard work has become her
and she has become hard work
to make a life a living
and a living of a life
in a world of inequity
and unfair advantage
where does she scale?
better not know
because knowing is worse than pain
worse than humiliation
so, i put in one head phone
and then the other
and music drowns out the reality
that as i begin my run,
that woman and i,
are the same

Behold, a Vanilla God...

the bud goes through the pain of opening
i should, too
for beauty to be born
we've got to walk through the hard things
heavy rains make us what we are
although pleasant, we cannot grow where we are sheltered
the wild is what wants us
the wild is what calls us
and if we are brave enough and accept,
the reward is a fragrant flower
the reward is who we are

VANILLA GODS

i wish there were a place for just you and i
a place where i could get to know you
all of you
the marks you got as you played a child
the rebellion you had as a teenager
the bravery as a young adult
and then the thoughts as you were my mother
i remember i would walk into your bedroom
as you put on your makeup
and that Red Door fragrance
i would watch you tentatively
this stranger i know so well
the pieces i got of you
were here and there as you went about your days
other pieces
you'd leave in writing in those books to God
i'd envy him sometimes
you talked to him all the time
if given the choice to let God die and
leave a billion souls lost, to wander without their Savior,
just to know you,
if all of our wishes had conditions
then this is why most do not come true

if you go to the lake here in Malawi,
you will observe fishermen
and if you are like me,
you will sit in awe
small boys learn from their fathers how to fish
and those fathers, too, were once small boys
who learnt from their fathers
for many, this life is all they know,
the water stretched out is their prayers answered
their confirmation of God
a God that protects, nurtures and loves
the fisherman, i accept, although having stayed in one place
knows life more than i ever will
his paddle through the waters is his meditation
and if meditation be how we prepare ourselves for death,
the fisherman is a spectacle
to those of us who tremble at the thought

VANILLA GODS

my siblings are all i've got
people equally attached to the same woman as i am
sometimes, i think i am alone
until they come along and mention something
that let's me realise they've been thinking of mom, too
they miss her, too
we are one
beating in three
i will always love you guys
more than i envy you
and the time you had with her
i love you more than anything on earth

it's okay
I'm over you now
You're free to live your life
as you always have been
i don't expect any reunion
i let you go
i let you go

VANILLA GODS

i am aging
soon there will be crinkles in the brown satin seams of
my skin
that i was born into all those years ago
so smooth
like the wine i tasted before eighteen
now, teenage years aside
i am getting older
a little bolder
standing taller
as i dare on my dreams
and stand with eyes that gleam
a future
and revere a past
of days of joy and sorrow
i am getting older
not much time til the grave
but girl, be brave
and if you are to have any baggage
let it be a bag of ambition
other than that, be free
alone, you
are a wave in the ocean
and the cool wind through a house
and the dress of a beautiful young woman
you are that woman
no comparisons are required for you
unique unicorn
no, tiger
i am getting older
chin up
standing taller

with a heart that is forever young

VANILLA GODS

dear lover,
let's run to the waters
and dance in them
hold my hand
we are free
the sun is ours
the yellow orange glow of its ascension
and then the blue of the sky
it's a good afternoon to be silly
and wild
let's run to the waters
I'll kick my feet through the sand
laughing harder than ever
this is beauty
perfection
uncontested proof of a God
in these perfect moments

dear valedictorian
you've collected so many trophies
if only you could have collected
many manuals on how to do life, too
because no one knows
and that is what you will learn now that you
will put down your books and look to the real world
there is no book that perfects a formula
to life
we all just speak of intangible things
and concepts we cannot summarise
but dear valedictorian,
in your cap and gown,
when it comes down to it
there is no greater intelligence
than that of love
and that is the truth

VANILLA GODS

mother used to enjoy milky tea
in a cup she'd take from the drawer
she didn't have any favorite cup in particular
that's what i most remember
she would take any of them,
without bias,
as she was with strangers,
and friends,
offering them her heart in its fullness
like they were all equally deserving,
and in the cup, she would place a teabag into it,
fill it with hot water
and then the milk
oh god, the milk
which i so strongly opposed
being a child with my own particularities
milk, i hated, especially the cream
but mother could put her finger in the cup
collect the cream and eat it like it was the
most delicious thing in the world
apart from wanting to make me gag at the sight of it
whenever she made a cup of tea
i'd be filled with joy
because of her gaze as she stirred into it
and then she'd put it to her lips
every sip was a meditation for her
never had i seen her more happy
with all the sadness
her life knew
these were the rare moments of joy
and she'd tell some jokes
forgetting about everything with that cup

i'd watch her move to the step
just outside the kitchen door
the sun setting casting an orange glow
very much similar to the yellow orange in her cup
and i would be held in all that vibrance
as she, too, was held in those moments, thinking whatever
she was thinking
a smile on her face, sometimes,
God, the heavens know,
the heavens know,
that i understand now,
how clouds can break into a rain giving storm
over and over and over
because this is what becomes of me whenever
i think of you
the words i miss you are not enough
but are all i can say

VANILLA GODS

i like vanilla as a color
i like vanilla as a scent
i like vanilla ice cream best
when i make anything, i use vanilla essence
i like vanilla in my fingers
i like vanilla in my hair
i like vanilla in my bedsheets
i like vanilla in the air
i have fallen so in love with it
it's all i can think about when it's not there
i like to think about vanilla
but mostly, i love that vanilla doesn't care
it demands feel my presence when i'm here,
here, there, everywhere and always,
have yourself a vanilla love affair

vanilla as a color
vanilla as a scent
vanilla as a lover
vanilla as a friend
vanilla as an obsession
vanilla as a drug
vanilla as a saint
vanilla as a thug
vanilla as a liquid in a bottle
or vanilla, nice and raw
vanilla is more than just vanilla
vanilla helped me cope

VANILLA GODS

you drew the curtains closed
although the sun was out
and looked at me with a smile
then moved over with a certainty
you then plunged yourself onto the cream beddings
where i lay and i felt your weight above me
the bed became a sea
i felt i could tell the sceptics
'love is really real'
i too was once like you
but it's safe to believe
your hands ran themselves along my skin
their meeting so smooth
smoother than the wine you poured for me the night before
when i thought you would go
but the thing about love
is you don't ever want it to end
and that is how we moved from the dining room, to the sofa,
and then to the bed
now, i am blessed with your kisses
and the wetness of your tongue
with which you say your prayers
and praise me, like cicadas the sun
i'm buzzing from your love
my ears run wild with sound
when you have taken me to climax
and our movements accelerate, then slow down,
until we're finally done
but never ever finished
that's what this loves about
because you're the only person who ever stayed around even
after i showed my true self

it's a sweet kind of love
a blessing from the galaxies
there isn't a cell of doubt in my body
when it comes to you
and to this, all you've got to do is bring your hand
to my chest and let my heart testify

VANILLA GODS

i poured flour into our kitchen bowl
and added milk
then stirred a hurricane out of it
in the bedroom, your eyes were still shut with sleep
a world you travel to that i laugh at
when you murmur something in your sleep
i added some vanilla essence
to it, after the baking powder, and it clung
to my skin, the vanilla,
fingers you will kiss later, saying beautiful
i looked at the batter and then remembered,
i almost forgot the eggs
i cracked them in and stirred
funny, how things can fall apart when one thing is missing
that's what i feel like you are for me
the missing piece
and there it was, ready for the butter greased pan
heavens know i have gone through bitter moments in my life
but with you, i can sense i have arrived
at some wonderful place
which words fail to describe
you are what i was made for
when i was just a spec in my mother's womb
this moment
you
you and this tiny little house we call home

I am ready for my life
Ready for the mystery to unfold
Ready for misty mornings
Ready for my imprint of foggy breath
Ready for silver
Ready for gold
Ready for rosy dawns
for purple dusks
Ready for lightning strewn skies
For the daunting act of trust
Ready for walks up the mountain
Ready for the breathtaking views at the top
Ready for drives through the country
Ready to watch birds as they flock
Ready for my feet at the waters of the lake
Ready for conversations with fishermen
Ready for the secrets of good trade
Ready for lazy days
or laborious days under a scorching sun
Sweat beading my forehead
No escape from this galaxies sun
Ready for my commitment to care for earth my home
Ready for love
Ready for the season of spring
And winter if it should come
Ready to be a flower princess
Ready to be a winter bug
Ready for acceptance and rejection if need be
Ready for the truth ready for the lie
Ready to hold my breath and then let go with relief
But as much as I try,
I'm never ready for this

never ready for goodbyes

Some days we do nothing
And if you're like me that can get in the way of your self-worth
We tend to equate productivity with self-worth
But let me tell you something
something that I've learnt
Even when you are doing nothing
Millions of your cells are working to keep you alive
Breathing amongst themselves
Fighting against death
Just your breath
is everything
And that is miraculous
You are always worthy

VANILLA GODS

We're all part of some maths
written by a creator who is
surely intelligent
and naturally pays attention to detail
the more you pay attention to it,
the more beauty you observe
the unity
the belonging
simply in the length of your arm
even when we feel we fall short
we are part of something much larger than we are
so when i look at you
or a flower
or feel lonely
I realise that I am part of something
very, very, very,
oh my,
I can cry
something so holy

The fruit fly is in love with the wine
Not knowing that it is in love with the grape
That is me, with the stars at night, the trees, the glowing rising sun
These are all just manifestations of God
The fruit fly so charmed by the potency of the grape
Then flies so close to the wine that it falls in and dies one with it
This is what will happen to us all
Becoming one is going home to what we love
It is our destiny
Our purpose
Our fate

VANILLA GODS

we can make something positive out of
our brokenness
trust me, i know
i have seen things that maim the soul
disfigure hearts
and obscure sanity from the mind
but there is a way out
there always is
a way through it
to peace
you've just got to trust the deepest part of yourself
that holds the silent truth that you
are strong
capable
wise
and above all, beautiful
all of the mess is beautiful
even the mess that stripped you of the good things
trust me
just trust me
i have watched souls mend themselves from shatterings
ashes become something
for the sadness we have lived
there is a greater joy waiting for us

imagine if we always lived in appreciation
of the things we have
i mean everything
this thought dawned on me when my phone was stolen
while I was in a shop the other day
That phone had everything I needed
I didn't realise it had become my best friend
this thinking then extended itself out to everything in my life
the toilet roll, the clothes on my back, the bed I sleep in,
my laptop wherein I write, the accepting pages of my diary,
my sister, my brother, my friends, my family,
kind strangers, protection, peace,
good health
if you look, you can see how good life really is
to whoever it was that took my phone
fuck you but thank you, too
because you showed me life

VANILLA GODS

vanilla is not only a scent
but music, too
it drowns out the noise of a fucked up world
i put vanilla to my nose
and i hear the music play
it's stronger than the HIV, cancer
rapes, racism, sexism, famine and wars
for a while, it all makes sense
none of the bad things exist
just good, just this vanilla

I've heard the center of the universe
smells like blueberries and tastes like rum
So, on my birthday, I wished to travel to it
and I poured myself a glass and ate blueberries
The cheapest, weakest spaceship ever built
in my kitchen before I moved over to the living room
where I barefooted danced
to slow music
Forget meditation
Is rum and blueberries the quickest way to become God?

VANILLA GODS

The sun came up
And I went into the kitchen
I took a lemon and ginger root
Sliced the ginger root, and the lemon in half,
squeezed the yellow lemon of its juice into the mug
And added the ginger pieces,
then the hot water,
always piping hot water
brought it to my mouth and blew it cool
these are the remedies we do for our bodies
how we try tell them we love them
like our ancestors did more frequently
devoted medicine women
this is my humble offering to my body

sunflowers have their own sun salutation
this is what i think about as i do the
sun salutation
yoga pose
yoga has been there for me in ways i cannot express
when i once lost my head
and grew a tough neck
severed consciousness was healed
by a downward dog
upward dog
and sun salutation
like yoga, the sun has always been there for me, too
waiting for me to come into its alignment
and finally i have
and it feels so good
sanity restored
and beyond that, a new way of seeing
a new way of living

VANILLA GODS

to feel good, do as follows:
you need to do your nails
and your hair
and shave your legs, arms, armpits,
that delicate place
or if you want, let it all grow wildly
keep a clean home
fill it with nice scents
spray yourself with good scents
keep flowers around the house
listen to good music
cook with good spices
get a run every now and then
have good sex
drink wine occasionally
and detox lemon water
do yoga
say a prayer
dance, dance some more
laugh
jump on the bed
befriend a good-hearted person
read good books
watch fucking amazing movies
keep a dog, or cat
appreciate nature
gift someone
donate to charity
if you can, start or join something you're passionate about
do the above regularly and i can ensure you
you will start to live a life more worthwhile
when we look at each other as women,

we should not compete
but instead lift each other up and complement each other
then soon we will have a world of so many empowered women
that the earth will vibrate
and hum a tune of triumph
they once burned us
now, see the ashes of our ancestors rise
and rise
and rise
in us

wild African hair grows from my follicle
I am a beautiful brown woman
Black woman
I enchant with my hips
And flirt with my lips
my skin is covered in coconut oil
shimmering like the waters of a lake under the sun
I am an African woman
A beautiful woman
with a fine neck
and legs
and bosom and backside
Artwork
Art in my mind, too
thoughts and compassion for the world
I am a wild African woman
Mother to humanity
And yet, so often, treated as a slave
Excluded
Hands bound, mouth taped
But you can't get me down
Me and the soil that feeds you are one in the same
Without me, there is no you
For me, surely, the Creator has a destined place
I'm a strong, beautiful African woman
Go on, listen,
Mountains chant my name

I think to some degree we
all want to be seen as worthy
We all want to be appreciated
For people to see us as valuable beings
A perfect world for me
is one where each person is valued
And seen
and cared for
This is the Heaven on earth that is talked about
With devotion and discipline,
we humans can make it happen
All we've got to do is believe in it
and then commit to it

VANILLA GODS

Herbs communicate an understanding to us
How desperately they long to help us
If we allow them,
we could revolutionise earth
Heart by heart
Humans got it wrong
True wealth is our plants

In echo of a great writer,
I too once chanted God is Dead
My rationality, I would call it, for a while won the fight
But then one night,
it was really silent,
so silent you could go deaf,
and I was struck by this awe revelation
wherein I asked, Is that you?
And the response was It's up to you

VANILLA GODS

He held my hand
And we walked through a forest
Me, taken aback by all the trees
Trees for so long were my symbol of strength
My truest role models
So giving
I smiled and could have almost cried taken
aback by all the beauty
For once, a guy had done right
Had understood
Me
Had understood
that it's always the small things that matter
I felt afraid
How pleased my heart had been with him
So, I tried to pull my hand away
Return to what I knew
Being alone
But then he said, holding my hand still,
"It's taken you so long to do just what you were made for.
Breathe."

A long time ago
The Gods had a meeting
For what object they'd taken on possession
And manifest as on their time on earth alongside their creation
All the Gods showed up for the conference
And immediately began claiming,
'I shall be the rivers' one God said
'And I the oceans.' Answered another.
'I the mountains,'
'And I the volcanoes'
'I, an island.'
'And I the wind.'
'And I, the rain.'
All the God's claimed something to be and
eventually the conference was over.
As the God's were readying to leave, a gentle voice spoke.
'What about me?'
It was the youngest of the God's speaking.
'Oh yes,' said the oldest God. 'And what shall you be?'
The youngest God thought a while and then smiled.
'I shall be the Vanilla of the earth.'
And so Vanilla became a God.

VANILLA GODS

I heard that the stuff that's in my teeth
is in the stars
I have a smile of stars
And that is why when we smile at each other
we feel something
powerful
We are reminded that we are in the Heavens
whilst we are on earth
We are Gods, too
With a beauty that lights up the night sky
With us always, even in the day,
when the stars don't shine for a moment
You and I are so beautiful
Beyond what our minds can perceive
So always hold on
Hold on to that
And smile

There is a great joy that comes from
sweating
Dancing
Running
Skipping
Jumping
All acts that end in a sweat
Produce a beautiful feeling
of joy
and freedom
And an understanding that one is alive
Sweat is a gift from God
A sign that you are working with Creation
All your cells singing
beating
Hallelujah

VANILLA GODS

I saw him running
with his two dogs
and already my mind started dreaming up
things
His abs under his shirt, his firm arms
all holding me
His sensitive side, if he had one
I hoped he did
I mean he loved dogs
I could see him
that I needed him in my life
But I went the other direction
And kept on running
Someday, I'll manifest a good guy
My blues for love will be over
Because I deserve Love
Surely, I do

I learnt there was a God flowing through my veins
Two hours past midnight
A God that really loved me

VANILLA GODS

When people think of vanilla, they often think of white
But vanilla comes from the vanilla bean which is
brown like my skin
Black people are like the vanilla bean
Forgotten in the contributions they made to society
And then another takes credit for their work
They are humbly in the back, growing in the mud, doing all the labour
    Carrying the true essence
    The world thinks of me as less
    That is the truth
    Because I am a black woman
    But that is not my essence
    And that is the truth
    I am the vanilla bean
    Forgotten
    But it is I who makes the beauty
    I am the Vanilla God

Physics can try to explain these things
And interestingly so
But even physics knows that when the silence comes
It's left to say oh my God

VANILLA GODS

I once had a lover who was musical
He'd sing me songs in his beautiful voice
and every time, I'd travel to some surreal place
where the world was a dream
a beautiful dream
It was like taking some drug
maybe heroin, or cocaine,
but I don't know drugs
but I know that if anyone listened to it the way I did
listened to music from someone you love
you become so sure nothing could be as good as that
so good that you become convinced a God lives in them
sent to you to experience it

I combed my afro out
And you came over
We went dancing
Took shots of whatever
And moved our bodies against each other
Threw our hands in the air
Threw our worries, too
The funky music taking us with it
It's all so funny if you really think about it
We're just happy dancing skeletons

VANILLA GODS

I don't want to let you down
I want to love you right
I want to be so mature that I recognise you as a human
That I see all of you
That I am so in touch with myself and emotions
That I can't hurt you
I want us to be lovers
And I want us to be friends
But before you, I must befriend myself
I've never witnessed love that works before
To the point where I have my doubts
I killed the girl in me a long time ago
But something tells me, I need to bring her back to life
For us
I want to get this right
For a while, I kept myself from you
But I can't anymore
I'm in love with you
And I love you
And I guess I got a little scared
Because usually I am not afraid to lose people
But I don't want to lose you
And thing is I've never been afraid of being broken
But now I am because I want to be good for you
Loved by you
What I'm trying to say is
with you, I'm where I need to be finally
Everything is aligned
You are my ascension
All of my cells are alight
Which words would be the equivalent of a saxophone playing a seductive tune?

Those are the words my mouth needs to speak
Those are the words that my throat needs to feel
Those are the thoughts my mind needs to think
The words of the sexy saxophone
the union of beauty

VANILLA GODS

Take your coconut oil and lather your skin in it
Run it through your wet hair, too
Then take your knees and kneel on the floor
Bend if you must
Kiss the floor if you should
Put your hands in the air
Praise its creation
Mediating any situation
Remedying the imbalanced step
Worthy, oh worthy
Of this kiss
this kneel
these oils
How precious
to have met
the Vanilla God

I am tired of witnessing my sisters
suffer
Witnessing them be misused by the men they choose to love
the men their hearts fall for
I am tired of seeing my sisters cry
because they have been mistreated
ill-treated
I am tired of having my shoulders wet with their tears
from hours of weeping
witnessing the disbelief on their faces of how
they have been seared
by the people they thought they could trust
I am tired
So tired
Of these broken hearts, slumped shoulders,
bulgy eyes, distraught minds
which are meant to be beautiful
creations through which God shines
diminished women
hurt women
I am tired, oh so, tired
of little men
insecure men
and how the world's got it all so wrong that it is them
who should rule

VANILLA GODS

The broken heart of a woman turns to
money and dick
and somewhere realises these are the only things
that men are good for and the best things
My advice to women is live freely
fuck who you want
or don't fuck at all if that's what you want
take your bodies beyond pleasure
that heart of yours was never meant to be shared
hearts beat best for one person and that person is
you
spend money, too, on things you love
And then above all, talk to your God
Love your God
Choose your God
and worship it
and worship yourself, too

I learnt that I have a God in my head
and a second God that exists in between
my legs
I fed my head books
And strum my second God like it was a guitar
I realised that everything I ever need
I can give myself
I've got it all
And that left me so confused because then why
was this other gender created
that only wastes my time
if their nature was to
take and never please the second God
fear the first God
only destroy the perfectly
healthy third God,
my heart?

VANILLA GODS

I realise happiness is real
when it's Sunday evening
and my belly is full with good food
And I am now in the kitchen
washing the dishes
wiping the stove
My ring on the windowsill
Indie music playing in the background
The floor mopped clean
Loved ones chatting
And I smile
these are the precious moments
when you pay attention
that we are alive for
all of these little moments

My friends are good people who
help me shine light on myself
on the good in myself
they help me out of the messes
I sometimes find myself in
Steer me in the right direction
Are filled with good intentions
My friends are authentic souls
that I can't get enough of

I am beautiful
I decided it
I really am
I don't need anyone else to feel full
To feel good
I am so strong
I am the definition of a beautiful person
I take my pain and turn it into strength
I take my thoughts and make of them shimmering gold
I am beautiful
My, oh, my
I don't need no mirror
But even mirrors bow before me
they can't handle the beauty
the sincerity
the strength
the resilience
the spirit of this woman
who can't be broken
the spirit of this woman who sees
beauty in everything and everyone
this woman whose eyelashes are the sliver
of 10 000 illumined moons
this woman who is gentle like whatever is gentle
And strong, oh so strong
simply beautiful

I could sense that the cure was in the piano
At just 10 I knew
That there was something about that brown wooden thing
that sat in the music centre
Something about it for me
In the black and white
Pressing them down was like pushing against something in me
I understood that when in that room there was something dark about life
That I'd have to learn to do things that I thought I could never do
Like part from mother
So I'd send my fingers along the instrument
Foot on the paddle sometimes
That piano was so beautiful
With its darker notes and lighter ones
That was me beginning to learn some story
A story of how things go

VANILLA GODS

I realised late at night
that I had been living by some strange untruth for so long
that in order to love me, I had to be loved by someone else
Someone else had to see the light in me
And suddenly, it dawned on me
how wicked and perverse
that makes no sense
I am the person I've been waiting for
It's in my gleaming eyes I will discover true love
I am the lover
these arms
this nose
this mind
it's me

If herbs have companions,
then surely we do, too
some herbs just can't grow together
and I think that's what you and I were
we were incompatible
the soil was either too acidic for you
or alkaline for me
it was always just something
and I'm starting to think maybe that's okay
we just weren't meant to be
and that's okay
it doesn't mean we didn't try hard enough
or one of us was bad
we just weren't companions
and were never meant to be

I know a girl who lost to the devil:
It was my aunt
I know a boy who lost to the devil:
It is was my uncle
I know a woman who lost to the devil:
She was my mom
I know a girl who nearly lost, but had to claw
Her way out his grip:
She stands in the mirror
- Generational curses

Sweet daughter
Your intentions are beautiful
looking to help everybody else
wanting everybody to be okay
servitude makes up your spine
I get it
nature of selflessness
A giving giver
I see you running around
Running is the culture for you
The norm
But I see you're turning purple
out of breath
You've been running around making sure everyone's
fine that you ran out of time for yourself
Sit down, it's okay to,
I promise the world will keep turning
rub into your feet, put oil into those bruises
And have a moment for yourself

This may be my father's kitchen but I will cook you a meal like you are the man of the house. I may be a working woman but loving you will be my main job. They may say women are from Venus but for you I'll migrate to Mars. What I'm trying to say is I will go above and beyond for you.

To me, there is no glamour in being a warrior
We don't choose to be warriors
If I had a say, there'd be no fight
Life would be a beautiful beach on a warm
Sunny day

VANILLA GODS

My anger left me
Not all at once
But in doses
It was like it passed through an hourglass
Transforming first to grief
Then heaping up at the bottom
As love

Not all trauma ends with the victim making a 180 in healing and coming to love their perpetrator and that's okay

When a lover brings you flowers,
You do not cry out and say,
'Oh, why, flowers, they will be dead in a week'
You bring them to your face and smile and put them in water
With creation it is the same
This earth is its enchantment
The rising sun its charm
The wind its caress
The night sky a bouquet of flowers
You, its lover
Your life its kiss
When someone you love comes in for a kiss
You don't move away, you move in closer for the seal
So have no fear of where we go or the passing of time,
This is what it's all about
A dance
A simple kiss
The symbol of requited love
That is all that the end is

About the Author

Tamara Mushani is a young, black African writer who grew in Sandton, Johannesburg and has now relocated to the country wherein her parents were born, Malawi. She writes about the challenges the human spirit faces in grief as well as challenges for black people.

Milton Keynes UK
Ingram Content Group UK Ltd.
UKHW050647260624
444769UK00004B/140

9 798224 892181